The Poetry Of
John Ashdown-Hill

Copyright

© 2018 John Ashdown-Hill

ISBN 978-0-9945175-8-6

Published by
Maximum Felix Media
PO Box 440
Korumburra VIC 3950
Australia

Cover Design by C S Hughes
(Detail from a late 19th century bronze by F Coppa)

First Published May 2018
Reprinted 2019
All rights reserved.

Contents

12 Moth
13 The Rape Of Ganymede
14 Fairy Story
15 Le Labyrinthe
16 The Labyrinth
17 Soli Invicto
18 Καί ὁ Λόγοσ σὰρξ ἐγένετω
19 Mon Réve
20 Barking Tye
21 Maripaso
23 Dialogue With Myself
25 The Dreamer
26 Ὁ τοῦ ʽ Ηφαεστιόνος Θάνατος
27 Epitaph
28 Souvenirs De Valence
29 Souvenirs De Valence (English Version)
30 Soledad
31 El Afán
32 Leda
33 The Journey
35 Reflections on the Sea at Sizewell
37 The Hekate Night
39 Chaplet
40 Habit
41 Delphic Oracle
43 Before Departing
44 Epitaph For Dion

Contents

- 45 Images Of The House Of Minos
- 46 L'Ange De Noël
- 47 Portrait du Poète
- 48 Round Trip
- 50 On The Akropolis
- 51 A Letter
- 52 Seperandoci
- 53 Τῷ Ἀλεξάνδρῳ
- 54 The Island
- 55 Le Procès du Rocher
- 57 Jealousy
- 58 Contact
- 59 Voyage To Mount Athos
- 60 Separation
- 61 Imelda
- 62 The Mourning Of Achilles
- 63 Soliloquy For Helen
- 65 Agamemnon
- 66 Seeking
- 68 Pteranodon
- 69 Message From An Unknown Planet
- 70 The Lottery Ticket Seller
- 72 Night Flight
- 73 On Vain Love's Worth
- 74 Dream Of Mary Fenton
- 78 Fate Of The Gentle Singer
- 81 Euripides In Love

Contents

- 82 Midnight Recipe
- 83 Matthew Fenton's Wedding
- 85 Piègè
- 86 Aunt Daisy
- 88 Temptation
- 89 Soul Search
- 90 Sending Patroklos
- 91 Cinders
- 92 Caritatis Vestris
- 93 Recordando a la Eva Perón
- 94 Lady Of Hope
- 96 Apologia
- 97 A Sort Of Exile
- 99 Vision Of The Grail
- 102 The Stoning Of Queen Olympios
- 104 Memories Of My Grandfather
- 106 Board Game
- 107 Euripides On Salamis
- 108 Euripides In Macedonia
- 110 Reflections In A Glass, Darkly
- 111 Family Tree
- 112 Lord Of The Flowers
- 113 Reflections On A Romance
- 114 The Second Death
- 115 Evolutionary Trials
- 117 Baby Bird
- 119 Flying A Kite In A Thunderstorm

Contents

121 Boudicca's Farewell
123 By Alton Water
124 By Alton Water (ii)
125 Psychopompos
126 The Last Oracle
127 The Indian Chronicle 1. Nawab Ali
129 The Indian Chronicle 2. Indian Miniature
131 The Indian Chronicle 3. Conflicting Loyalties
132 The Indian Chronicle 4. Different Perspectives
134 Meeting In A Wood
136 Winter Garden
137 Coy Fruit
138 Waiting
139 L'Espoir du Pessimiste
140 Here & Now
141 Emptiness
142 Stages Of Possession
143 When I Write To You
144 The Quest Of The Holy Grail
146 Without You
147 Only Because Of You
148 The Centaur
149 The Tenth Of October
150 Time Factor
151 The Gate
152 Connections
153 Childhood Memory

Contents

155 Meeting The Need
156 To A Passing Dragon
158 Out Of Season
159 Name-Dream
160 Through The Desert
161 Brush Fire
162 Tranquilidad
163 ICU
164 Ghazal
165 Seeking Safety
167 Missing You
169 About The Author

The Poetry Of John Ashdown-Hill

Moth

O moth!
I thought you were a clothes moth,
Now you are a squashed moth.
Sorry, moth!

(Norwich, 1969)

The Rape Of Ganymede

I was alone, and glad to be alone.
He came to me,
Said: 'Come'.
His talons gripped me,
And my flock of thoughts
I left, bleating forlornly,
Shepherdless.

We flew,
And from the fields of my lone peace
He bore me up on pinions of desire
To high Olympos,
And I had no will,
But, vacant eyed, I gazed,
And, mesmerised,
Saw like a god.
And the world was little
And far away.

(Norwich, 1970)

For my return to the Church.
I had been brought up as a Christian,
but had stopped attending church in my teens.

Fairy Story

Shall I recount the tale from the beginning?
Tell of the fairies present at the birth,
Each Fate her gift bestowing on the child?

Only one, spited, uninvited crone
Sealed with a bitter wish my destiny.
Her spindle pricks my tongue when I would speak,
And seals, as in a castle, hedged about
With nettles, ivy, thick and thorny bramble,
The one important sentence I would utter.

At her behest I, through this age of life,
Must hope perpetually my long despair,
Till comes the final and relenting angel
Whose kiss, from gently smiling, parted lips
Shall drain both life and hope, and set me free.

(Norwich, 1970)

Le Labyrinthe

Les maigres quinquets, qui éclairent
L'espace vide de mes pensées,
Me protègent contres les furies
Qui dans la nuit
Viennent me dévorer,
Et sur la terre fâchée,
Comme Ariane, je danse devant la Mère
La labyrinthe de ma perplexité.
Le jeu est fait;
L'amour,
La vie,
La mort.
Je gage les poupées sacrificatoires.
A pas léger
Je foule aux pieds
Les cornes du ciel qui me secouent,
Les lèvres souriantes,
Les yeux fermés
Contre l'enfer
Qui m'est ouvert
Dessous.

(1973)

The Labyrinth

The flaming cressets light a little space,
Holding at bay the lurking dark;
Night's Daughters watching.
My feet, like Ariadne's, tread the angry earth,
Dancing the maze before the Goddess
With dolls of sacrifice,
Playing at love and life and death,
Light-stepping on the tossing horns of heaven
With smiling lips,
Eyes closed to the abyss
Which gapes below if I should step amiss.

(English Version, 1973)

Soli Invicto

Oh that you would come,
My Beloved,
Rising swiftly on the wings of the morning,
Treading the dawn.

(Undated – c.1974)

Καί ὃ Λόγοσ σὰρξ ἐγένετω

Cloud-like, I floated through a vault
Of black, where no sun ever shone.
Like vapour from the swirling water
My note sang forth across the gloom,
And I shall pierce the turning circle,
Descend the whirlpool to the womb.

I come, I come, and are forgotten
The boneless hands that rolled the sun.

(Undated – c.1974)

Mon Réve

Je rêve toujours à toi;
En songes je vois
Comment on se repose
Dans un jardin
Bien garnis
De lys
Tous blancs,
Et plain de roses.

(c.1974)

Barking Tye

I conjured you today to walk with me
Along a wooded path
Where jade sunlight
Paved the ground with dappled lace.
A tunnel, almost,
Where only the trees behold.
Saw your face smiling up at me,
A sending only,
- Of your heart or mine?
Oh, that your own desire,
Not the compass needle
Of my too-fond imagination,
Gave me a while your presence
More real than memory too often recalled.

(1975)

Mariposa

In hues of gold the sunlight fell
On jasmine-scented flowers,
And palm-fronds green umbrellas spread,
Magnolia blossoms, shimmering red,
Embraced the perfumed hours.

And from the sky of dreaming blue,
Through day, bright crystal light,
On iridescent wings came by
A many coloured butterfly,
Breeze-blown in aimless flight.

Upon the sea of glassy blue
Beneath the flaming sun
With sails of white a white boat gleamed,
In poppy-scented breezes dreamed
Its aimless course to run.

Wind-born, the lovely butterfly
Across the water passed,
And as, on flickering wings it flew,
Beneath the same breeze gently blew
The boat's sails at the mast.

The boat beheld in dreamy thought
The butterfly descend.
Two aimless, moving, breeze-blown things;
Wind filling sails, wind lifting wings;
We are alike, my friend.

The butterfly came fluttering low
To settle on the stem.
We are alike. I'll stay with you!
It said. But the wind stronger blew
And separated them.

(Málaga, August 1975)

Dialogue With Myself

He was part of my dream, of course - but then I was part of his dream too.
Lewis Carroll, *Through the Looking Glass.*

Are we a dream in the mind of Deity, or is each of us a separate dreamer evoking his own reality?
Gore Vidal, *Julian.*

I close my eyes and there we are
Together, you and I,
Shut in, apart from everyone
In isolated union
That is not unity.

I thought that I perceived your Thought,
The Thought that conjured me,
The dream you dream of me, a speck,
A mote that moves upon the tide
Of your Eternity.

I know you are my prisoner,
Though I can find no key
Nor means to break into the cell
Where I have held you life on life,
Yet I must set you free.

Shut in, apart from everyone,
Mutual imprisoning.
Through endless aeons we have dreamed.
Are you my thought, or I the fruit
Of your imagining?

(Ipswich, 1976)

The Dreamer

– life, what is it but a dream
Lewis Carroll

Be not importunate,
And quietly tread,
Lest he should wake,
For he has dreamed me well
Through many thousand ages.
Let him sleep,
And sleeping, dream,
That he may safely bear me
Beyond the final setting of the sun
Unto my last horizon.

(c. 1976)

Ὁ τοῦ Ἡφαεστιόνος Θάνατος

What can I give you, greater than the Gods,
If he is gone?
No art, no thought of mine
That could assuage that pain.

If he is gone? – Is he not gone?
Wherefore in black,
Stripped of their gold and rainbow hues
The seven-fold walls of Ecbatana mourn.

Yet while I dream, - and other,
Faithful too,
    -You have him still.
I dream of you together.

(1976)

Epitaph

I was a word
Spoken in darkness.

Before that mind conceived me
And breathed me forth
With bloodless voice
To drift a little while
On the winds of the world,
I was silence.

And now the shape of flesh
Those fleshless lips have uttered
Has rounded to its final syllable,
I shall again be silence.

(1977)

Souvenirs De Valence

Tes cheveux noirs
Devant la fenêtre de minuit.

Tes paroles s'envolent
Dans la chaleur de la nuit
Comme la fumée des cigarettes.

Dans ce pays d'hiver
Je reste seul;
Le verre vide sur la table.

Et même le souvenir me trahira,
Puisque j'ai tant de fois vécu
Dans ma mémoire
Cette heure perdue.

(1977)

Souvenirs De Valence

Dark hair
Against a midnight window.
The wisps of smoke curl away,
Glasses sit empty on the table.
A southern night
Where warmth endured.
In this winter land,
A southern night
Where warmth endured.
In this winter land,
Your warm presence lost,
I am the drained glass.
Your words,
Ephemeral as smoke,
In wayward curves evade my memory,
Since I have lived that hour so many times,
Changing the dialogue to fit my dreams.

(English Version, 1977)

Soledad

Un grito oscuro y torcido
tiembla ahogado en el cuarto vacío.
Tic-toc; mi corazón,
Tic-toc; el reloj.
Soledad
y la flor seca de tu indiferencia.
Mis alas oscuras de necesidad
se golpean contra los cristales de mi ventana
en busca del eco lejano de tu sonrisa,
y las horas pasan despacio.

(c.1977)

El Afán

Las víboras de la noche
me muerden otra vez.
Estoy envenenado,
me retuerzo,
y la pared y la cruz delante de mis ojos
se funden, como el hierro frío de mi corazón
que tú has endulzado.
¿Por qué has puesto el afán,
esta serpiente vieja, en mi pecho?
Estoy herido,
y el hilo rojo de mi sangre
se disuelve en el agua negra.

(c.1977)

Leda

What profits it to struggle?
Or how could you withstand
That white and feathered on-rush;
The great and beating wings,
Those gripping feet, webbed, black,
The biting beak
That battens on your breast?

(1978/1989)

The Journey

– si lunga tratta
Di gente, ch'io non avrei creduto
Che morte tanta n'avesse disfatto.
Dante, *L'Inferno*

Beyond the wall of stones, but not alone,
I walked into the dry and silent land,
Each step about my feet the dust clouds rising.
And down the long and cinder-covered slope
Through debris of eternity descended.
Beheld, in the still dark above my head,
The coldly flaming, unnamed constellations,
Stars that the living eye had never seen,
Which, glittering hard in that unending dark,
No sun has ever shamed, no moon diminished,
No drifting cloud concealed from the beginning.
The stars which give no light, but only serve
To magnify a thousand times the dark.
My guide before me walked, a jagged figure,
The robe a hollow joke to cloak the bones,
Shaping the nothingness into a body.
He led me through the dry and silent land
Where water does not flow, and breeze not play,
Past rocks unweathered, mountains sharp as pain,
And brought me, so, at last, before the Queen.

Sometimes a spider form she wears, and weaves
About her endless webs of shrouding darkness,
Her cobweb nets to trap the hopes of men,
Which food she craves, of which she spins unceasing
The silence and the blackness that she loves,
Her night that knows no dawn. Sometimes a lady
Tall and pale and perilously fair
She stands in robes of black. She is the Mother.
All men are her children, from her womb
They journey forth upon the many paths
That are one path to lead them all to her.
She has no love for men, and mocks their prayers,
But draws them to her on a diamond chain,
That they may all adore her and despair.

(1978)

Reflections on the Sea at Sizewell

Ti sei mai chiesto dove vanno i vecchi dei che il mondo ignora?

I know a sandy beach
With sea foam crashing,
Where, with a stick upon the salt-drenched strand,
I wrote a few words of the ancient tongue
For the oncoming breakers to devour.
There, once upon a time, I walked to hear
That soft, immortal music touch my ear,
And see the endless, rolling surf, that bore
Upon a raft of floating scallop shell,
The nascent Aphrodite to the shore.

I seek her now,
As I have ever sought
In all, or any of her many guises,
The Many-named.
Shall I go once again, - and vainly still, -
To where her white birds sail the empty sky?
Though in the stirring of the white-flecked sea
I hear the echo of the Cyprian's voice,
Not here, nor on the strand of any shore,
For all my restless seeking,
Will she come.

How shall man steer a path between the gods?
The sacrifice withheld is not forgiven.
So I somewhat Hippolytos' crime
Must likewise expiate,
Who, having to her surrogate
The lesser offering denied,
Was by a wall of water overwhelmed
Among the pounding breakers of her womb,
And by the greater sacrifice appeased
The only fair, to see, at last, her face.

(1978)

The Hekate Night

Black dog howling,
Throat open to the sickle moon
Where two roads cross.
Flying clouds of night
Show the thin sliver of light,
Sharp as pain;
Thin, cold moon,
Warmth craving, blood craving,
Life craving.

I am the cold moon in the hand,
Sharp, thin edge of brightness in the hand,
Freezing, hungry blade in the hand,
Warmth devouring, blood devouring,
Life devouring.

Let me in, black dog,
Freezing and thirsting.
I am the bright moon sliver to your open throat,
The thin root of howling.
I am the sickle sweep
To reap your warmth.

Beat the earth to the powers below.
In darkness greet the powers of night.
Black dog, quivering on the ground,
Speed to your mistress.
Warm blood, spurting on the ground,
Soak to the womb.

(Ipswich, 1978)

Chaplet

I love her only,

> As the flower is plucked.

I love her only,

> Holding in my hands
> This petal pack of cards,
> The shuffled fates.

I love her only,

> Playing out the game.

I love her only,

> As the petals fall.
>
> And has my love a name?
> A whispered breath
> Sighs all the seeds away.

Her name is Death.

(Ipswich, 1978)

Habit

O, all the earth is lost in habit now.
The waves have crashed
How many times
Upon the beaches of the mind?
The sun has risen and will set,
Winter, again, will come with snow
And go.
All this I know.

I would like Alexander live and die,
Burning away
The day,
The life, the body's clay,
Fuelled with new sights, new visions,
Until, with joy, I come to Babylon.

(1978)

Delphic Oracle

Through spun grey shadows, cobweb nets,
And night mists rising from deep pools
To thread fools' diamond drops on gossamer,
A cold wind blows, shredding the scattered veils.
A voice, like beaten bronze, says: 'Know yourself'.
The burnished metal mirrors subterfuge.

No man can make a child know all his mind.
Before the god each man is like a child.
Apollo Loxias, the Double-Tongued,
Uncoils his thought along the python's trail.
He knows, he warns, we fail to comprehend,
While in the dark his words move to their meaning.

So on the hare the eagle stoops
With hooded crest and pinions spread.
The sickle talons harvest blood.
Sun arrows of the Unforesworn-of-Tongue
Unfailing home, and swiftly cleave the mark.
Lay bare both conscious and unplanned deceits.

Yet his own mist veils all his purposes.
The smoke that owns divinity
Weaves clouds around the Navel Stone.
How can man know what Truth is to a god?
Feel the dark smile behind the riddling answer.
Of this be sure: he does not mean what you mean.

(1978)

Before Departing

The soul remembers good, but cannot see
Through clouds of deeds, its immortality.
Will you remember, in the Cretan night,
And strive to beat the fallen wings in flight?
'Ω ἐρώμενος μου, shall I put on

Achilles' armour for the fate fore-known?
Smile Plato's smile again to speed your ship
Across the sea to bloody Syracuse,
Put honour first, and join the souls in one?

The god, his hounds unleashing, cries them on,
And baying in pursuit they swiftly track.
Long was the hunt, and devious the flight.
So I have struggled on the pin of fate
Till I am spent, coursed down, and in the net.

When you are far away in space,
As lost in time is unity,
Hearing the echo of the surf
That ebbs no fickle tide away
But beats with proven faith upon the shore,
Cry to the sea: «μαζί, μαζύ».
For oh, to face the darksome voyage alone
When even Alexander could not bear
Divinity, without Hephaestion.

(Summer 1978)

Epitaph for Dion

Now lies in blood the hand you would not soil
With base necessity.
And but a little while and all is dust
That breezes bear away,
But honour shall be yours eternally.

From youth to man, seeking the Good through Love,
In Plato's steps you trod.
You stood before us on Parnassos' slopes,
An image of the God,
The dream personified, in royalty clad.

Syracuse called you forth, and Plato patterned
The role for you to fill:
Do good: better to suffer than do evil,
Better to die than kill.
You pass the test, and you are Dion still.

(1978)

Images of the House of Minos

An ancient house between the crimson pillars
Corrupted by the sun-fire in the blood.
The lingering desires of Pasiphae,
Unnatural lusts behind the jewel-bright walls.
The subtle poison, hovering in the air,
A two-edged blade that battens on the skull.
Now ruined beauty, broken Anthedon,
Mown down the budding spring-flower in the heart.
The silken web, spun by the Ancient Ones,
A Cretan Maze to trap the Lily prince.
Accursed the house that like a warning wears
The patterned brightness of the renamed snake.

(Summer 1978)

L'Ange De Noël

Nous avons fait un ange ensemble,
    -Toi, la tête, et moi, les pieds.
De toi les ailes pour s'en voler,
De moi les mots sacrés,
Comme, entre nous,
C'est toi qui vole
Et moi qui écris les paroles
Que je n'ose pas crier.

(Christmas 1978)

Portrait du Poète

Je ne suis guère poète, et ma chanson.
N'est que le crie
De la Nuit
Contre le jour dont elle est privée ;
Contre l'aube qu'elle hait.
Elle n'est que la complainte
Du noir, qui n'est rien,
Contre le blanc, qui est la somme
De toutes les couleurs.
Elle n'est que l'orgueil de la lune pâle,
Qui n'est, enfin, que l'ombre du soleil.

(1979)

Round Trip

Three waited for me on the farther shore.
The hank Lachesis held,
This I had been.
In Clotho's hands the new, soft fleece
Gave me my choice.
I chose.
Twisting the spindle in her Mother's lap
Atropos twists the pattern of the thread.

Walking back the dry way
Through unshaded light,
Blistered lips whispered over searing sands.
Sharp needle points, unweathered, slashed my feet.
The light and love the body could not bear
Burned me to the parched dry parchment shell.
So at the river I drank deep
The waters of Forgetfulness,
Purging my mind of the unwanted brightness.

And now I damply rot,
Living the aches I took upon myself,
Twisted into the pattern that I chose.
Here on this hither shore I wait,
Nails pressed into the palm,
Clutching the last coin in my hand,
Fare for the boat to take me home.

(1979)

On the Akropolis

Come, walk with me
Where friendly shades,
Thronging the shimmering air,
Tremble in silver haze the olive leaves.
Tread upwards the sparse green
Spread on burnt ochre
Where, floating in the sky of painful blue,
Yet rise the mellow ivory bones,
The ruins of the jewels of Perikles,
Which the High City still uplifts in worship,
The phoenix rising from the Persian fire.
Beyond the reach of time,
To glimpse, maybe, beneath the shaded columns,
The saffron flicker of Aspasia's gown,
Or catch her lingering perfume on the air.

(1979)

A Letter

When first I came, I thought I could not bear
For so long not to see you.
My time seemed an eternity to live through.
The newness, and the strangeness, gave me first
Other, and lesser thoughts to occupy me,
But habit grows upon me, and I weep,
Silently, and inside, - as all my thoughts
And feelings for you have this long time been
Silent, imprisoned in the marble tomb
Which is the face necessity imposes
I show the world and you. – What pain it is
To walk beneath the sun and not to see you,
To tread this soil your feet have never known,
To feel a breeze which has not touched your cheek
And breathe this air which has not passed your lips.
Imprisoned on the hard horn of the world,
The slowly circling heavens only bring me
Another dreary morning without hope.
So slowly wears the weary time away,
Until the bitter day when we shall meet
And talk again of little, pointless things,
Leaving, as we have always left, unsaid,
The glorious impossibility
Which fills my sleeping and my waking dreams.

(Florence, August 1979)

Seperandoci

I came with seeds of hope
Which slept a while in the uncertain spring,
Reaching, at last, for the brief, smiling sun,
To late to come to fruit.
The chill, unseasonable weather
Now blights the hopeful buds with sudden frost.
Now I have plucked the bitter herbs
Of this day's parting:
Laid them on the bier
In place of all the sweet bouquets,
The flowers of rare and delicate perfume
And rich and varied colour
We might, together, have gathered,
Which now are left unplucked
To bloom and fade and wither unobserved
In that fair garden we no more shall see.
My hair is shorn and twined into a wreath,
Crowning the pyre and waiting for the flame
Which shall consume and turn to ash
The hopes and disappointments
In one brief, potent paroxysm of pain,
One last, bright warmth before the winter comes.

(Florence, September 1979)

Τῷ Ἀλεξάνδρῳ

'When all is said and done,
You are not quite like all the others'.
These words you gave me long ago,
And in another tongue.

During the time, we raced to meet the Gods
Have you forgotten?

The white horse, once again defeated, falls,
The dark steed drags us down,
Back, for a while, to wallow in the mire,
This mud of matter.
Always we fall, and fail.

I was with you, my Lord, in Babylon,
And I in Egypt served your tomb
As I grew older and you stayed the same.
Do you, like history, now forget my name?
Yet I am bound to serve you,
Life on life
I follow you through birth on weary birth.

(1980)

The Island

When we were children, you would say:
Come with me,
I'm afraid to go alone.
And we would go together
Sharing out
Courage and fear between us.
But at the last step do not bid me come,
For though you fear,
That bed too narrow is for company,
And you must go alone.

(1980?)

Le Procès du Rocher

– quid feci tibi, aut in quo contristavi te?
Responde mihi!

-	Os de la terre,
Je me tiens tout droit;
(C'est le rocher qui chante.)
Je fais parti d'une grande falaise,
Qui en été et en hiver
Se baigne les pieds
Jusqu'aux genoux de pierre
Dand la mer.
Par beau temps il me fait plaisir
De voir le va et vient
Des oiseaux qui viennent nicher dans mes bras.
Je les protège contre la pluie, le vent.
Ma fermeté leur donne confiance.

-	J'accuse ce faux rocher,
Faux et perfide qu'il est,
(C'est maintenant le pauvre oiseau qui parle.)
Comment aurais-je pu savoir
Au printemps, quend il m'a fait bienvenu
Qu'une fois venu l'hiver et les tempêtes
Il m'aurait brisé
Contre sa façade dure ?

Le rocher maintenant reprend parole :
-     Si, par beau temps, tu te repose
Sur ma fermeté,
Que tu prennes conscience également
Que cette fermeté, par mauvais temps
Soit aussi fort danger.
Ce n'est pas moi qui change,
C'est la saison.
Moi, je n'ai point changé.
Tu dis que je suis dur,
Mais que sais-tu,
Être de chair et sang,
De ce qui peut faire trembler la pierre ?
Et qu'as-tu vu,
Toi qui s'en vole sur le vent,
Pris par les frissons d'air,
Des larmes de la terre ?

Et toi, qui passes
Sur le chemin,
Ayant écouté,
Juge
Entre l'oiseau
Et le rocher.

(1980?)

Jealousy

O crudelis Alexi, nihil mea carmina curas?
nil nostri miserere? mori me denique cogis?
Vergili: Ecloga II

The hemlock ache spreads numbly through my veins
Seeing the laughter flowing from the bottle,
Sparking from glasses
The borrowed shine in eyes
Or wit on lips.
The curling dance has caught you,
Takes you from me.
Your eyes go with the laughing feet.
I tread, alone, in darkness,
The twisting menace of the Labyrinth;
My horned fate waiting at the final turn.

(Thessaloniki, August 1981)

Contact

Warm, your arm
Brushing against my arm,
Remains,
And does not shrink.
Firm, your hand, and gentle,
That does not fear to touch my flesh.
My eyes caress again
The golden body,
And, leaning close, I scent the wholesome fragrance,
Sweet smell
As of warm cake, fresh baked,
From your bare body drifting,
Or clinging to your clothes.
The distant, mist-blue eyes,
Jewel-shocking
In the golden face,

(Thessaloniki, 1981)

Voyage to Mount Athos

Λάμπει ὁ Ἥλιος, ὁ Θεὸς φωτεινός
Δόξα στὸ γαλάζιο οὐρανό.
Τὸν βλέπεις καὶ σύ,
Ἂν καὶ ἀπὸ μακρυά.

Στὸ πλοῖο μου γλιστρῶ
Κάτω καίεται ἡ θάλασσα,
Πάνω καὶ ὁ οὐρανός.
Φλέγομαι καὶ ἐγώ,
Ἡ καρδιά μου καίει γιὰ σένα.

(Thessaloniki, August 1981)

Separation

My eyes are storm clouds
Dark with rain
In the tempest of departing.

My eyes are beacons
Flashing mute messages
Through the storm.

My eyes are windows of memory
Struggling to retain you
As you slip away.

(Thessaloniki, 1981)

Imelda

Grey and gold in a crimson chair,
Brow clear, and eyes with wonder glowing,
A tall and slender sunbeam by the open window,
The lodestone to my gaze.

The child I sometimes am for you
Walks at your side through crowded streets of noise,
And you, the finger tips touching,
Make it a dappled glade of forest sun.

Or I will be the man, but not myself
But what you make me,
Wielding a power of earth, air, wood and water
That breaks me and reshapes me.

(Canterbury, September 1982)

The Mourning of Achilles

μονου γαρ αυτου και θεος στερισκεται,
αγενητα ποιειν ασσ'αν η πεπραγμενα.
Agathon

Wolf cry,
Dog howl of desolation.
Jagged metal,
Sharp, torn edges,
Rasping the throat.
Splinters of glass
Shoot into fingers grasping earth.
Mud,
Where Skamander meets the sea,
Stops the mouth
The writhing body drives into the ground;
Salt mud
Where the empty eyes have passed,
Turned inwards
To the parting
When he bore away on his shoulders
Your glittering guilt:
Looking over the outward sea,
Seeing the inner vastness,
Chasm of grief
Through which you fall forever alone.

(1982)

Soliloquy for Helen

- ιω ιω παρανους Ἑλενα.
Aiskhylos, *Agamemnon*

Is it for me they fight?
What's it to you, Greek,
Who has soft Helen,
That you should train your bloody entrails
Across Skamander's plain,
Clutching at eyes
That drip like bloody tears
Down furrowed cheeks,
Feeling the slender leaf of bronze
Tear through the flesh
And grate against the bone?

Too late now,
Brother Agamemnon,
To weigh the bitter cost of honour.
The dear blood paid
Binds you beneath my walls.
Meanwhile my sister
Gathers the fate-threads in her hand,
Weaves you a purple cloak
To bruise the earth,
To bruise your feet.
Weaves you a netted shroud

After so long,
Menelaus,
My stranger-husband,
Grey creeping in the ginger beard
Brings dreams of Helen's breasts
Sagged ten years lower;
Pictures the fair face
Scarred by the churning chariot wheels,
Lined with every sword-thrust,
Etched by the double grief,
For Troy, for Greece.

And I can no longer tell
How I came here,
Only remembering how the soft talon
With nails retracted
Gathered me up in its velvet embrace,
Then sank the scimitar claws
Deep, deep into my breast.

(1982)

Agamemnon

Walk on, proud man.
Feet that trampled the altars of Ilion
Crossing the little, dusty square of home,
Treading on crimson
To where the shining death behind the door
Sweeps down.

(1982)

Seeking

I shall never waste my life-span in a vain useless hope,
seeking what cannot be.
Simonides

This is not it,
Not this.
Give up,
Accept what comes,
Praising the lesser good
Nearer to hand.

This is the outward, Christian resignation
That goads the pagan soul within,
Raising the feathered vanes
To beat away
Upon the Isis search,
More hopeless yet
Because the goal unknown.

I knock at each fair-seeming door;
Sometimes one comes,
Yet not the sought unknown.
Sometimes the house is empty,
Or else, for all the door be fair
There dwells within
Some dreadful thing
Born of the outer dark,
Eager to batten on the dark within,
And, feeding on me,
Like a cancer grow.

Driven on,
Driven on by the fear
And the longing greater than fear,
Finding good men, not perfect,
Not the soul's mirror
To show, not what I wish to seem,
Nor yet the image,
Blurred, and much distorted,
That others have, who cannot comprehend,
But the self in another,
Knowing the thought before the mind conceives.

(1982)

Pteranodon

What eyes can now discern that distant sky?
Out of man's reach beyond the unicorn
Since all the earth was changed,
Where snow-white, sleepless wings untiring sped,
Now melted into stone.
No breath of hot, aspiring air
Rising from arid canyons of your seas
Stirs passing shadows of the vanished waves
Above which, hung on silver webs
From long, imperial fingers spread,
Lord of the sea-sky, born of wind and clouds,
With grace unparalleled you rode the air.
For on a distant day,
While I and all my kind were yet unborn,
You died; cold bone lying beneath the rock.
Hard stone now mocks the backward seeking eye,
And aching grief bruises the longing heart
That I may never see your matchless flight,
Nor hear the echo of your lonely cry.

(1983)

Message From An Unknown Planet

Would you observe me?
Analyse
And classify my constituent parts?

I am flaming rock
Where your feet may never stand.
Swirling, poisoned colours of hot gasses
That you can never breathe.

I am, throughout the sun's burning,
To your unmarked occurrence
And small decline.
Awaiting not your eyes' beholding
To put on perfection.

I am myself,
Though you were never born.

(1983?)

The Lottery Ticket Seller

Every day she stands
In the Plaza de España.
«Números para hoy.»
Her speech has some impediment,
The words break from her with an effort,
A slur of sound
Crashing into my heart.

There is a booth nearby
For lottery ticket sellers,
But here too there is hierarchy
And she stands open to the wind and rain,
Twisting against the weather
On wet days
To keep her paper numbers dry
And cry
Against the wind
«Números para hoy.»

And each day as I pass
- She knows me now
By sight -
She smiles
And I with lips and eyes
Smile back
And inward weep
To see her standing there
And hear her cry
Like jagged metal thrust into my heart.

(Bilbao, November 1984)

Night Flight

You conjure, and I flutter coloured wings,
Frozen and aching from their long disuse,
Through night less dark than days of poppy dreams.
Then I dozed, sun-warmed; scented nectars tasted.
My tongue, uncoiling through the day's bright sweetness,
Marked not the bitter drug beneath the flower.
Cold dark awoke me. Iron petals closed.
With dagger tip, day blossoms bruised my lips.
Bone-chilled and hungry through the dark I fled
To where the star-fire at your wand tip gleamed,
With diamond images my path bestrewing,
And my night-darkened eyes, that sought the light,
Homed, through the shadows, to your flame-flower haven.

(January 1988)

On Vain Love's Worth

Rusticus es, Corydon; nec munera curat Alexi,
 nec, si muneribus certes, concedat Iollas.
Vergili: Ecloga II

Touch my mouth with violet glances,
Opening the heart
Singing in the silent centre of the stone,
And let me prodigal my love's profusion
On your indifferent altar.

The songs that sang in silence shall be heard,
Rock-bound before.
Raise now in the still sphere the surging storm
Although your ears be deaf, and your enchantment
Be careless worked.

So sun, unmindful, scintillating, sets
Aflame the icy diamond
That in the earth millennia had slept
Cold, dead and dark. Yet, fired, true nature shows,
For all the sun's uncaring.

(February 1988)

Dream of Mary Fenton

Crescendo in the head,
Wrath rising.
Trapped in family,
Crushed by needs of children,
Husband, neighbours.
Prisoner on this flat and distant shore,
Heart swells with mountain longing,
Tabla pulse beating in the blood,
Soft santur throbbing.

Oh, to be again
The father-bereft baby
Born on high and distant hills.
Dark eyes, first opening on the world,
Turning to pristine and untrodden snow
White-glistening on the slopes of Nanda Devi.
Rest the mind
On the high places of girlhood,
Dark hair of the land in the breeze flying.

Born, poor child, with conflict in the blood.
The dark hand
Wrenching the bitter sabre upwards
Through your father's throat
Is your hand,
Though the colour does not show.
The agony spurting from his dying lips,
Unheard by you,
Is your cry.
His, your anguish.

So, white lady,
Dark-eyed lady,
Black-haired lady,
You of the oil and vinegar blood,
Casteless and homeless,
Of uncertain race
And place,
Wandering far from your birth land
In the cold, damp country of exile
They told you was home,
Trapped, trapped,
And the impotent wrath
Beating an alien rhythm in your head,

How should you not long to be free,
Walking, in the clear, upland air,
The high mountain passes
Of long ago?

And your blood in me beating
Bears to me across the years
The rage in your heart.
My mind, too, moving
In Asian rhythms.
I would bring you peace,
Poor, long dead lady,
Feeling your anguished soul
Still writhing in confusion.
So I have set your image in my mind
Again on white, Himalayan slopes,
Beside a pilgrim shrine
You knew, perhaps, long since,
And I have seen you, in my picture, smile
And be, at last, content.

(February 1988)

Mary Fenton, born at Landour, India, in 1846, was my great grandmother.

Fate of the Gentle Singer

Την ψυχην, 'Αγαθωνα φιλων,
επι χειλεσιν εσχον·
ηλθε λαρ τλημων ως διαβησομενη.
Plato

Flower, fallen in the frozen north,
Faded petals frittered on the wind.
Locked, the lips
The quivering soul of wise love longed to trespass,
Stilled, the song.

Shoot, silently nurtured
In the south sea-city,
One in growth
With the shining temples
Of the gold and ivory maiden.
Schooled by silver-bearded Sicilian wisdom,
While the sour poet, hermit on the shore,
Who pierced the grandiose solemnity
Of subterfuge
To the bitter meaning at the heart,
Soft-handed you through calf-love.

Fair spring blossom
Laid on the Wine-Lord's altar.
Star that shone
In the shooting comet's tail,
Blazing a baleful trail across the heavens,
Flaming, fed on popular acclaim,
To fail, fuel-less and falling.
Then set free,
Orbit the steady rock of wisdom
Cleft from the Navel Stone,
And mirror to men's ears
Songs of the crystal spheres.

Wealth, wit and wisdom, prove
Lodestones of little envy.
The sharp friend
With acid in the smile
Stirs mud-wrath in the lees of home's rich cup.
So wisdom in a draft of poison sleeps.
The glass that showed men's meanness

Northward takes its flight,
The sight
To shuttered eyes
Too clear, too bright.
And you, too, gentle poet,
In the far north shall sing
Your lost, forgotten swansong
For a young, ill-fated king.

(March 1988)

Euripides in Love

Ηρα θε φασι, του αυτου Άγαθωνος τουτου και Ευριπιδης, ο ποιτης, και του Χρυσιππον τό δραμα αυτω χαρισόμενος λεγεται διαφροντισαι.
Aelian

Over the purple blue following,
Where on the anchored isle,
Whose sun sparks stars from spangled rocks,
You circled in the dance,
To the bright god the clear voice raising;
And in the bays
Your golden brightness bare, the water cleaving,
I spied.
Black spines, the salt blue upward piercing,
Shafting my foot
Like arrows of the god,
The blood threads, cloudy, through the bright sea curling.
So nature overcomes my intellect;
Urges the Laios crime within my breast.

(March 1988)

Midnight Recipe

Your tawny silk
My kneading fingers blend
In lumps of pleasure,
Stirring the drops of after-midnight darkness
With ripples of your laughter,
Seasoned with little breaths
And pillow murmurings,
As, upward-curving to the gentle movement,
First loins then shoulders arch.
Then, from the concentrated
Summit of your breasts,
My circling hands diffuse
A gentle heat, dissolving,
Eyes closed,
Your features in soft smiles.
And when you will
I cup you in my palms,
Raising you softly to my waiting lips.

(August 1988)

Matthew Fenton's Wedding - Cawnpore March 1843

That bright spring day
From Flagstaff Barracks as you made your way
Through dusty Kanpur streets
To new-built Christ-Church,
What distant flicker was it caught your eye?

Only, perhaps, the sun,
Like flames that flicker,
Glancing upon the face of Ganga Mai
Where dust clouds, near the Sati Chaura Ghat,
Arise like smoke against the morning sky.

Discreet behind the houses,
An unseen Bibi Garh,
Where underneath
The noises of the street,
Some children cry.

A frisson of cold breeze, this wedding morning:
Pain premonitions, shadow of a sigh.
Which of your wedding guests could read these signs?
See looming fingers of the lurking Fate
That in the Black Year, for them lay in wait?

Nor you, a little older
Than, when he passed this way, the Golden Boy,
Foresee in heat your feet his footsteps tramping;
Your body cut beside the Sutlej River,
Your veins red tributaries to its flow.

(February 1989)

Matthew Fenton, who was killed in the First Sikh War, before the tragic events of 1857 overtook Cawnpore, was my great great grandfather.

Piègè

The many-coloured surface spirals down.

Deep in the midnight centre
Currents flow,
Swift, uncontrolled.

Beneath, Medeia-like,
The mind in torment twists to wound itself,
And, crab-wise, grows
To fit the shape that outward things impose.

Poor, frightened thing
Squirrelling in the net
That, more it round, evading-would, enmeshes.

(February 1989)

Aunt Daisy

Behind your eyes
A heavy veil
That masks today,
And here, and now,
While through the gauze
New people come and go.
'You must, you know, do what they say'.
And here's an aluminium tray:
Your lunch;
And: 'Eat it while it's hot.
'I know it's early,
'Not much past eleven;
'But then, your surname starts with "A" '.

The doorbell rings
For meals-on-wheels
And nurse
And social services,
Yet you will say
'Nobody came today'.
And rightly so. For in your mind
These busy ants are nobody,
And those that you would wish to see,
The somebodies,
Are dead and gone,
Or rarely come; live far away.

So, meanwhile, in your mind
You wait,
And with your silver button hook
Your boots secure,
Or, shaking out
The many frills of petticoats,
You take your father's hand
To walk
To Lady's Mile
And see the coach
With jangling team of four go past
From London, as it brings the mail.

Not deigning not to dwell in yesterdays
Of sharper vision,
Still un-aided ear,
And many peopled love that round embraced you.

(April 1989)

Daisy Naomi Ashdown,
1890-1992, was my great aunt.

Temptation

Sed et serpens erat callidior cunctis animalibus terræ...

In midnight woods,
Deep, deep in hidden pools
Where, in the dark,
My serpents drink or bathe,
I glimpse your face;
See how my flickering tongue
With ripples troubles your serenity.
Beware my smile!
These subtle lips, that send
Soft, rosy apples at your innocence.

(May 1989)

Soul Search

τοιάδε κύκνοι ... συμμιγῆ βοὴν ὁμοῦ
πτεροῖς κρέκοντες ἴακχον Ἀπόλλω.
Aristophanes, *Birds*.

Swan Lord, dance with me
On water, necks entwined.

I have no song,
I am the silent bird.
How shall I seek you?

Find me the hidden land,
The tearless time.
Land-lock the world and words.

In secret rites
Seal me from lips and eyes.
White breasts; my pillow.

Let dying but to you
Unlock my tongue
And teach me how to sing.

Teach me my swan song.

(May 1989)

Sending Patroklos

My love, my darling,
I'm afraid.
Take my place,
Bear my load.
Love pays all.

I've been insulted,
Sit and sulk.
Lift my burden,
Do my work.
I am yours.

This market love
I bargain with,
Devour you with,
Consume you with,
Barters your life.

My soul, meanwhile,
Is turned within,
Dwells on self,
Weighs the cost,
With stolen treasure
Pays the price.

(May 1989)

Cinders

The hurrying minutes tick away
And days that limped through heavy tasks
Fly, since I saw you, with unseemly haste.

Unknown, you bid me to your ball.
I, under some enchantment, came.
Minds, meeting there, and intertwining, danced.

But in my ears already sounds
Midnight's first stroke, that breaks my spell
And in your heart leaves but my velvet footprint.

(May 1989)

Caritatis Vestris

The Little boat draws near across the water.
I would embark,
Not hear your good advice,
So who will slip the coin beneath my tongue?
Not gold, nor silver,
Copper will suffice.
I am already near my destination.
In pity spare a penny,
Pay the price.

(May 1989)

Recordando a La Sra. Dña. María Eva Duarte De Perón

El relámpago cae
desde el cielo.
Se encienden las llamas,
reluce el fuego
que, cuando se quema,
centellea tanto.

Pero sube el humo
en nubes oscuras
y todo pasa
dejando cenizas.

(Mayo de 1,989/2,017)

Lady of Hope

Estas cosas pensé en la Recoleta
en el lugar de mi ceniza.
José Luis Borges

Behind the Recoleta's doric gate
The silent streets of quiet people sleep,
And black, and nameless is your marble tomb.

The daily flowers of love are still impaled
On iron spikes, to wither in the sun.

Yet through the living city streets,
In icons pale, from walls you smile.
Adoring stones in paint proclaim your fame.

The daily flowers of love are still impaled
On iron spikes, to wither in the sun.

And in poor hearts, that understand
Your vibrant, all-embracing heart,
Still, after more than thirty years
Of army boots, and guns, and death,
Your rainbow arches through the stormy sky.

The daily flowers of love are still impaled
On iron spikes, to wither in the sun.

(May 1989)

Apologia

I did not choose the path I tread.

Hand me a box, then, lock me in,
Or file me under G or H.
Teach me new words I did not know.

Like you I am unique, divine;
The spark of God is in my soul.

I never asked that you should understand,
More than you understand the sun,
The breath of life, the rose, the cross.

I move, like you, not knowing how
Or why, through time. I think and feel.

The bitter doom awaits us both
And tips the wormwood in the wine.
I make my way as best I can.

I tread the path I did not choose.

(May 1989)

A Sort Of Exile

Peacock on the wall,
Speak to me of my land.
Brass cobras, silver and ivories,
Speak to me of my land.
Silk pictures, and faded photographs
Of sepia Simla, shikaris and syces,
Speak to me of my land.

I hear a loved voice,
Soft and old,
Wreathed with scents of pipe tobacco,
Deep in an ancient leather chair,
Telling me tales of elephants,
Of soldiers, parades and Durbars.

Oh my land
Where my people lie
In graves erased
By monsoon rains.
By fumbling fingers of creeper felled.

Sparkle for me with mountain snows
And jewels and silk.
Put on the flowers
Of gold-mohur trees
And wear for me
Flame-of-the-forest in your hair.

My land
That my eyes have never seen,
Where my feet have not stood,
I hear your voice
In remembered notes of 'Zakmi Dil',
In the santur's sigh,
In the tabla's throb.
Oh India,
Aap mere mar-bap hãi.

(May 1989)

Vision Of The Grail

Being, for all these reasons, free from fear, I will write in this book what no one who has happiness would dare to write. I will accuse the Gods.

C.S. Lewis

One cup, lamenting,
Alone in the black.
Chalice of gold
Floating in the void.

'I was the vessel
Destined for the Great Feast.
For this were my ores mined
In the depths of time.
For this I was beaten,
Gauged with sharp tools,
Tortured with fire,
Abrased,
Etched with acids.

Prepared,
Ordained
From before the beginning.
Chosen to receive
The sacrifice of love:
The crimson flow,
Fairer than jewels
In my burnished depths shining,
My high adornment.

High King
Who made me
To be Love's altar:
Ark of the Covenant,
House of Gold,
Now I am empty,
Abandoned,
Forsaken,
Alone in the dark.
I am lost,
Alone'.

And I saw in my vision
The cup to me turn
Its bowl.
A void,
Gold-bounded and vast.
Black and deep
Beyond hope or eternity.

I drank from its depths
The blackness,
The coldness.
Deep, bitter draught
That filled me with emptiness.

You made me for love,
Lord,
I am alone.

(June 1989)

The Stoning Of Queen Olympias

Queen Olympias dons a ring
Of polished garnet framed in gold;
Threads her ears with shining tendrils
Clustered with berries of Indian rubies.
Descends the stairs in a waft of late summer,
Scents of strawberries, damsons and grapes.

Cloudy her jewels when she married Philip.
- Mysteries of Samothrace; dark in the cave.
Opals and amethysts,
Envy and hate.

Her stones, though, flamed on the day she bore
Divine Epiphany, lightening's son,
Alexander, child of heaven.
Diamonds and goldstones, colours of fire.

And what jewels did she wear on the day she killed
Eurydike and Arridaios?
Sapphires and emeralds, colours of poison,
Turquoise, chalcedony, lapis from Babylon.

Queen Olympias lies on the shore
Surrounded by stones like mounds of crushed cherries,
Streaked with crimson, streaked with purple.
Fire in the head and hate all around.
Salt tang from the sea, and the scent of blood.

(June 1989)

Memories Of My Grandfather

Your voice, your image fill my mind
Though it is long now since you died.
I have your height, I have your build,
Yet you, to me, are taller far.
Although I am not what you wished
You are my measure and my guide.
Imagination fills the gap
Of the lost years I did not know,
And in my dreams I see you stride
Through Simla streets to Annandale,
Or, solar topi on your head,
I watch you after blackbuck ride.
Through the bazaars I follow you
To perfumed Bibikhana nights
Where, through the air, on sitar strings,
The tinkling hands of nautch girls glide.
Your portrait hanging near my bed;
Work of your hands surrounds me yet:
Pictures and maps, calligraphy,
The toy you made once for a boy.
But in my ears I hear the drone
Of little insects bearing death.
The frightened child within me, still
Stands at the sick bed where you die,
And through the years, with heart and hands,
I tend your name and memory.

(June 1989)

My mother's father, Gaius John Ashdown, 1870-1955 – he eventually died of malaria which he had caught long ago in India.

Board Game

Sors immanis et inanis, rota tu volubilis.

So life,
This chequered parquet,
Brown and yellow,
Lays down
Possible moves,
Establishes
Constraints. Categorises
Colour; type.
Makes me patrol
My dark diagonal,
While in my ear
Fate speaks the unlucky number.

(Würzburg, July 1989)

Euripides On Salamis

Γέρασε ἀνάμεσα στὴ φωτιὰ τῆς Τροίας
καὶ στὰ λατομεία τῆς Σικελίας.
Σεφφέρη, Εὐριπίζδης Ἀθηναῖος.

My hair and beard are long and gray,
My skin grows mottled, old and blotched.
Time takes its toll. Alone I pace,
- For now I have no friends at all, -
The silent sand, the secret shore
Beneath the sky bereft of gods.
Across the strait the city gleams,
Holding vainglorious prayers aloft.
There, through the multifarious pricks
Of little minds, I learned to flee
My fellow men, and felt the lash
Of ignorance and mockery
Even from those who, with my words,
Paid the fare home from Sicily.

(September 1989)

Euripides In Macedonia

*ἔλα, θὰ σὲ πάρουμε
πάντα σύντροφό μας
στὸ μακρὺ καὶ ἀτέλειωτο
στὸν ἀργὸ χορό μας.*
Constantinos Hatzopoulos, *Dance of the Shades*

Limping in the north mountains
Under the dark trees
In my old age,
The Wild Lord came to me,
Bursting the circumcastellation
Of my perception,
Bidding me: 'Dance!'

On his winter breath
I am the snowflake, whirling,
Aping the April antics
Of apple blossom falling.

My shuffling will surrendered quite.
He shaped my arabesque,
Twisting my old frame to his music.

Bursting the shell of my frosted head,
Tendrils of smoke, blossoms of flame.
Leaving the dead and empty seed husk
Drifting, mindless, in his train.

(September/December 1989)

Reflections In A Glass, Darkly

Oppressed by walls, I gaze.
My eyes, confined,
Turn gladly to reflection;
False perspective.

Against night's blackness,
In the window, see,
Feeble and dim,
The echo of my room.

And I perceive
This shadow semblance true,
For it is empty
Where the curtain hides me.

(October 1989)

Family Tree

Καλότυχοι οἱ νεκροὶ ποὺ λησμονᾶνε
τὴν πίκρια τῆς ζωῆς.
Lorentzos Mavilis

The living face the future;
Look ahead.
All this is nothing to me.
I gaze backwards.
My thoughts are with the dead.

The growing, laughing child
Comes not to me.
My sap runs rootwards;
I, a barren branch,
Hang leafless on the tree.

Dreary, I aimless tread;
Shuffle my feet
About my empty house,
And through the rooms
Seek the beloved dead I long to meet.

(October 1989)

Lord Of The Flowers

So the young god
Who walks on flowers
With silent footsteps stealing,

Child, beautiful,
With arrows armed,
In the darkness stalking,

Now baits the trap
With midnight eyes
Beneath soft hair
Like faded corn,

And with your hands
Sinks in my heart
Again
His barb, his dart.

(February 1990)

Reflections On A Romance

Something swells
In the heart of the rose.
Hip or canker?
No-one knows.
Inside my head,
Twisting and turning,
That fragile thing
Which lives without learning
Broods on the page where I left the tale:
Where a fairy prince from his love receives
A treasure rare, a jewel beyond price,
Dropped casually into his hand as he leaves.

(February 1990/March 1999)

The Second Death

I live now in two hells, for I have lost God and live also without love, or without the love I want, and I cannot get used to that either.

Rose Macaulay

It was not meant to be an easy journey.
They told me at the start there would be stones,
And there were stones. They said there would be thorns,
And there were thorns. I yearned to reach my goal,
But not to set one foot before another,
And in my thought I leapt on paper wings,
Borne on swift zephyrs to the journey's end,
Rich images my mind intoxicating.

Temptation feasts on the compliant will
And waxes, vampire-like, as it grows pale.
There was a voice inside once, that protested,
My ears, when I was young, discerned its warning
Which years of disobedience now make dim
As I have trained my hearing to be deaf,
Turned from the path and wandered where I would.
So, having now lost all, both faith and love,
I stand afraid and lonely in the dark.

(March 1990)

Evolutionary Trials

I'd like to meet an archosaur,
For what they're like I'm not quite sure.
Their blood is either cold or hot.
Their brains are small – or maybe not.
There are so many types of these:
Some live in swamps, some climb up trees,
And some have wings, but cannot fly
(Or maybe never thought to try.)
Triceratops lives in a herd,
But some have feathers like a bird.
The plesiosaur is like a seal,
Or maybe a gigantic eel.
It lives in waters salt and hot,
'Like Loch Ness'. Says Sir Peter Scott.
The Brontosaur was a disaster;
No beast became extincter faster.
Its body was too large to heat,
Its brain, to small to move its feet.

It lived beneath a lake, perhaps,
Where pressure made its lungs collapse,
And when on land it made a trial
It moved, legs splayed, like crocodile,
Dragging its belly like a slug
Along a furrow specially dug.
Its limbs were always dislocated.
Was ever creature so ill-fated?

(I wrote this poem – when reading all the controverse speculations regarding dinosaurs – in the 1970s – date not recorded – and rediscovered it in 1990.)

Baby Bird

You cried to me
From beneath the sage.
A plaintive sound
On a single note.

Long legs, stubby wings
Too small to fly
And an open mouth
With a yellow gape.

You ate the worms
I dug for you
But still you cried
And I feared for cats,

But the cardboard box
I put you in
Was angular. Bare
As a hospital ward,

And I think you'd prefer
And understand better
A garden death
Among the flowers

Than a nurtured life
In an empty box.

(May 1990)

Flying A Kite In A Thunderstorm

I sought tall shafts with purple poisoned bruises.
Would kiss those stems that green umbrellas spread
High over cowering primroses and violets.

Behind the eyes, deep in the brain
Gathered the storm clouds bearing rain.

So thin the veils I wove about
The dark flame licking at my heart.
Three times I heard the fatal thunder rumble.

My webs were thin and tattered shreds.
My head filled with familiar dreads.

The bud, tight-clenched, is stifled by its scent.
The petal muscles ache with self-containment.
A bitter fist, brandished against the storm.

No warmth to bring release, no sun,
The sky is dark. I trust no-one.

Yet for you two, who too have sought
Cold shelter at the hemlock's heart,
I'll spread in sight of all the tell-tale colours.
Seeing your fingers, small and unprotected,
Struggling to keep afoot beneath the storm,
I'll shelter you, and laugh at lightning.

(May 1990)

Boudicca's Farewell

Azure amazed
The wide Ikenian sky
Stares down.

Beside black water,
Wolfbane.

I break,
- And see again
A temple fall in flames, -
The fluted columns
Flecked and veined with purple.

Taste the numb death
That hovers at the lips.

Do off the twisted glitter
Circling the neck,
And from the head release
The fiery skein,
Colours of blood,
Colours of flame.

Yet I lived forty years and more
In quiet,
Doing what women do.

(August 1991)

By Alton Water

Deep under trees
Blue shade.
I sit
And seek the water sound,
Softer than silence.

(August 1991)

By Alton Water (ii)

A young group,
They came.

Red beard, long hair
Threw stones at a can,
While black jeans and T-shirt
Fenced with a stick,
And they, all of them, laughed,
And some smoked
In the sun,
In the afternoon

But the pain in my knee
Reminded me:
'Soon you will be forty-three'.
And the pain in my heart
Said: 'You are alone'.

(August 1991)

Psychopompos
(a sleepless dream of childhood)

Empty head lies hollow;
Nothing outward stirs the sight
Of eyes out-staring from the bed.

From beneath the blanket
A hand reaches out in the dark.

The hour is chill: white unicorn.
How far is it to Babylon?
Beyond the mountains of the moon.

The child, when the winged god fled,
Would conjure help,
That older hands should smooth the hair
And lure him again.
This is a comfort past, and turned to dust.

Now that prayer
Has turned to prattle on the lips,
The madrugada emptiness,
Chill, black and silver,
Like a cloud
Enwraps and penetrates the mind.

Seeking Hermes, Guide of Souls,
A hand reaches out in the dark.

(October 1991)

The Last Oracle

Many come.
Much is gone; all is ruined.
What remains
Is admired, not understood.
Worship is another thing.
Tripod is lost, and Navel Stone.
Who now can find the sacred Spring?
Earth has triumphed.
Mountains awe,
While art and reason crack and fall.
Through many riddles, twisted words,
One voice speaks clear,
And that, the last:
'Take this message to the King:
The God has now no dwelling here.
Fallen the house, silent the spring,
Withered, the sacred laurel, and bare'.

(October 1991)

The Indian Quartet

1. Nawab Ali

His words, his hair, fell softly, darkly.
From within a hand reached out,
His mind an open door.

Most would have seen, perhaps, but dollar signs
Flashing in his dark eyes at my light skin.
In India all is muddled and confused,
And many-layered onion truth, unpeeled,
Only reveals an emptiness within.
Better to keep it whole. So I accept
That this, at first – always, perhaps – was part.
Yet there was something more.

I build him now into my memory,
Dressed yesterday in white, today in black.
In a garden, by a lake,
He stands in a pavilion,
Leans on a marble balustrade.
Or he leads me through the winding
Alleys of the Moslem quarter
In pride of home, despite the strife,
His city, green within the pink.

Still with soft tones and understanding
Where Maharajahs turned to ash,
Beside the Chhatris at Gaitor,
As we fumble through confusion
Of God-cursed, after-Babel language,
He holds out friendship and compassion.

But in my mind, most, last, forever,
I will see him leaning back,
Shoulder against his rickshaw's silver hauda.
As time runs out and language fails,
He twists the canopy's long tinsel tassels
In shimmering knots about his arm.

(Jaipur, December 1992)

2. Indian Miniature

Three times I made him laugh
On the road from Jaipur to Agra.

My little driver,
Perfectly in proportion.
I watched with fascination
His exquisite hands on the wheel;
Caught in the sunlight
Red glints in his lush black hair;
Admired the perfect profile,
Jewelled eyes, flashed in the mirror,
And sweet smile.

I asked him: 'Fatepur Sikri, kitna dur?'
Why did I fight so hard
His lack of English
With my mangled Hindi?
I probe in retrospect my mystery,
And only see – or I will only say –
That I would have him warm to me.

Three times I made him laugh.

The first, about the time
He took to have a pee:
Then, later, in the afternoon,
When he drove me again –
Which was not in the plan,
But was his offering to me –
He laughed when, beset by souvenir sellers,
I tried to persuade them to sell him postcards.
The last, though, was the best:
When I told him what he already knew:
That there, on the right, was my hotel,
And he snapped back in Hindi
As to a friend
That he jolly well knew
Without my help,
So I made a sad face
And I said 'Sorry!'
At which he clapped me on the shoulder
And laughed.
I knew then that we were friends.

So much communication passed between us
On the road from Jaipur to Agra:
Three times I made him laugh.

(Agra, December 1992)

3. Conflicting Loyalties

In Agra, nearer to Ayodhya,
I, who in Jaipur liked a Moslem lad,
Then came with Hindu friendship on my way,
Here see unmasked the bitter face of strife.
I walked with Hindu friends at evening
Down beside the River Jumna
In the shadow of the Taj
And in the distance saw the smoke
Arise, straight columns in the dusk
From three cremating corpses near the Fort
Where, through long years in his royal prison,
Broken-hearted Shah Jehan
Gazed at Mumtaz across the water.
Here, in the shadow of the domes
I found a little Hindu temple;
Ringing bell and incense rising;
Evening puja for Lord Krishna.
Here an old man spoke to me:
Said to me that I looked Hindi,
Seeing, perhaps, some little part
Of the past, or of my heart,
And spoke with honour of the vanished Raj,
But spat with hate at Akbar's race and Moslems,
And would tear down the Taj.

(Agra, December 1992)

4. Different Perspectives

He asked me my name, and told me his
Was Bahadur, and for thirty rupees
He begged me to take his rickshaw, for
A trip to the tomb of Itmad-ud-Daula.
The season, he told me, was very bad,
And yesterday he had only one tourist,
So I took him on, and he made me ashamed
As he worked so hard while I just sat.
He waited for me while I wandered round
The Moghul splendour Mahrattas burned
And Lord Curzon, as always, restored.
Then he cycled me back, and I longed to say
As he struggled up hill: 'I'll get out and walk.
Don't worry. I'll pay you anyway'.
And now I feel certain I should have done,
But I wasn't sure he would understand.
He left me a while at the park by the Taj,
And he trusted me, though I hadn't paid.
Then he took me back to my hotel
And on the way showed me a little house:
'I live here, sir, with my father and mother,
My brothers and sisters, my wife, and our baby'.
He asked me to stop at two shops and look.
'They will give me money for bringing you.
You don't have to buy, just go in and look'.

His honesty deserved reward,
So although I had no intention of buying
I hope I put on a good performance.
At parting he shook my hand and thanked me
And hoped for a better day tomorrow.
I doubled his fare, and I ask myself now
Was there nothing more I could have done
For a man so honest, who works so hard,
And is in such need, and who thinks of me
As wealthy beyond his wildest dreams?

(Varanasi, December 1992)

Meeting In A Wood

Nel mezzo del camin di nostra vita
Mi ritrovai per una selova oscura,
Che la diritta via era smarrita.
Dante, *Inferno*

Because I do not love you,
Because your absence opens
No chasm in my breast,
No Tantalus
Unsated hunger gnaws me,
No abyss
Of black and empty yearning hollows me
To a dying carapace
Eaten by a worm.

I can stand with you again
In the same, secret place
Beneath trees
Green with lichen,
And take my pleasure at your company.
Hear from your lips
The clues that sign your mind,
Or, as our heads, over some leaf or flower,
Lean close together,
Spice my eye-lids
With tingle of your ginger hair.

Meanwhile we both
Dimple the damp, woodland air
With a clear spring of laughter,
And afterwards we talk for a while
Of funguses and plants,
Of travel, lives and people
And places that we know,
Until, in different cars,
To different homes we go.

(February 1993)

Winter Garden

In my garden, snow is falling.

My voice,
A fountain,
Fights the creeping cold
With tinkling, bright droplets.

The daffodils that charmed you
Huddle, appalled beneath the snow.
Winter has come again.
Behind the closed blinds of your eyes
I feel you poised to go.

Cold,
And the sky is grey.
My lips, conceding,
With gentle, pointless words and tissue kisses,
The soft and flickering wings of butterflies,
Send you away.

In the hollow of my head
A numbness settles
In great, white flakes.

In my garden, snow is falling.

(March 1993/February 1999)

Coy Fruit

There is a blush
With which the peach
Signals its longing
To be plucked,
Invites the open mouth,
Lips on soft skin,
To melt its flesh
Into sensations.

(March 1993/February 1999)

Waiting

My bed,
A wide, white field:
Sheets
Spread for writing.

I lie alone at night,
Lit by the dappled light
Of fretted lanterns,
Behind brocaded curtains
And lowered purdah blinds.

Like Danae in her brazen tower
I still await the miracle:
Love,
Falling in a golden shower.

(April 1993)

L'Espoir du Pessimiste

Comment es-tu,
Ô mon ami
Que je n'ai jamais vu ?

Demain tu recevras ma lettre,
Feuilles de nacre
Salées de larmes.

Je veux te voir.
Un battement du cœur
Et l'heure s'approche.
Moi, j'ai peur.

(Juillet 1993)

Here & Now

In the silence of my room,
Your laugh still flickers on bright wings.
And I am happy, for you came,
Painting my house's memory.

Things that before were commonplace;
My daily life, me to myself,
Seem new, and strange as things unknown,
For I am changed, of different worth.

Though you are gone, my solitude
Sounds for me now a different note.
My heart is every moment lifted
By those little words you spoke.

(July 1993/November 2017)

Emptiness

Time passes,
And I feel
A vacuum within.

Just like a palace
When the court moves on,
My eyes now turn in
On an empty throne.

I only seem to hold a picture
Of my Lord
Who now is gone.

(July 1993/November 2017)

Stages Of Possession

You took me first
In dreams,
Before we met,
I, silently concurring.
Later, in words,
You told me of your needs.
I bowed my head, consenting,
When first alone together,
Though you, I think, were shy,
Your tongue,
Your lips,
Your hands
Were bold
And gladly took possession.
So now it needs
No dream,
No word,
No presence,
But, night or day,
Whether I wake or sleep,
You hold me fast
And I belong to you.

(July 1993)

When I Write To You

You left me pregnant,
Thoughts swollen
With the seed you planted.
I labour to bring forth my mind
In blood-stained lumps of words,
These half-formed things,
New-born,
Crumpled and red,
Held out to you
With tenderness and fear.

(July 1993)

The Quest Of The Holy Grail

An image
It might be,
Conjured by Queen Morgana
From the sea
Where shivers
Turquoise and pink
Tremble beneath the sky
Of blushing nacre.
A promise
Like an enchanted sword
Held high above the water
To call us on our quest,
Our long adventure.
A vision,
Shining white,
Of faery domes
And towers and pinnacles,
To which,
But only after many years,
We might, if we are worthy,
Come at last.

Fearlessly, if need be,
Ere we set out,
Winding the magic horn,
Morgana's gift
At Christmas, to the king, her brother;
Horn
That will not sound
When blown by a false lover.

(August 1993)

Without You

A black and heavy cloud
Floats in my head,
Billows behind my eyes.

My jig-saw puzzle body
Longs for yours
And shapes itself
To fit your missing form.

My mind,
By bitter silver seared,
Perceives
Through pain,
Time,
Torturer and enemy.

(August 1993)

Only Because Of You

Μόνο γιατὶ τὰ μάτια σου μὲ κοίταξαν μὲ τὴν ψυχὴ στὸ βλέμμα.
Maria Polydoure

Only because you talked to me last night
The day is warm and bright,
My heart is light,
Only because you talked to me last night.

Only because you listened when I called you
I slept the whole night through,
The sky is blue,
Only because you listened when I called you.

Only because you always will be there,
Because when everything is dark, you care,
Laughter and tears we share
Only because you always will be there.

My life has meaning, something strange and new,
Only because of you.

(August 1993)

The Centaur

Dawn light, when I awake,
And you, the Centaur,
Man-stallion, wise but powerful.
White teeth, strong limbs
And subtle hands subdue me.
I am the naked hero from a frieze
Prostrate before you.
This image, fixed, of our relationship,
Carved on a block of marble long ago,
Is both my ikon and my paradigm.
Rising upon me like the morning sun,
You turn your head,
Send forth your note of triumph
Piercing me through, the while,
Shaking my being
Which echoes after, echoes like a field
When hoof-beat thunder passes over it.

(August 1993)

The Tenth Of October

October
Ten days gone.
A quarter-year has passed.
Before,
Alone beneath the sky,
I piped thin notes
In praise of what I did not know,
And, in my longing,
Thought myself half beast.
But when you brought me love,
Through you
I knew myself a man,
And found my voice.

(October 1993)

Time Factor

Now I can hold you in my arms,
Shelter you from present care,
And for the future, promise make
That, while I live, I shall be there.
But I cannot reach back into your past
To ward off bygone years of fears and tears.

(October 1993/November 2007)

The Gate

A private gate,
Open to me alone,
Leading me through a garden
Full of pleasure,
To a strong tower
Where I can rest secure.

(October 1993)

Connections

Meet, talk,
Laugh, love,
Part.

When speech is movements in the air,
Words are shadows on a page
And writing, just a dirty mark.

But sometimes there is you:
Your hands, your lips,
Your silent closeness in the dark.

I feel the lack of you when you are gone:
Cold spaces in my bed
And in my heart.

(March 1999)

Childhood Memory

Alone at night, I lie awake
Finding myself a child again.
No friendly hand, no voice wards off
The little lurking self within.

The mellow, red-brick walls of school
Rise, nightmare-like, imprisoning.
I fight the hated place and time
But am constrained, remembering.

My hands, my mind, begin to shake.
Engulfed by fear, I see his face,
I hear his voice. Behind my eyes
I feel the sting of burning tears.
Although I know I want to cry
I cannot let them fall.

As I am pierced I feel the pain.
Trapped in my throat, the silent scream
Condemns me and proclaims my guilt.
Inside me broken sentences
And words collide: I should have fought,
Protested, struggled, run.

How could it happen more than once?
I twist and turn. My mind, on fire,
Reduces me to slag and ash
In my own eyes, and worthless trash.

How will it end? For still he steps
Inside my head against my will
And, unopposed, possesses me.
He has no right. I want him gone.

I cannot hate him, even now.
Is that defeat or victory?
Shame dominates my mind, and guilt.
(In daylight, friendly voices urge
Against it, but I feel to blame).

A balding pate may now replace
His ginger hair of seventeen.
We'd pass as strangers in the street.
How could he recognise in me
The boy who trembled in his hands,
Still whimpering within?

(April 1999/January 2004)

Meeting The Need

You hand, your voice, your open door;
Treasures of gold for me, and pearls of pleasure.
I think you would not ask for their return.

And if a little joy-warmth burned in me
Fuelled by the paper gifts left on your table
(Meeting your need. Worth more to you than me?)

Why douse that glow with calculating buckets
Drawn from the icy waters of repayment
When you may find one day a better way?

(December 2003)

To A Passing Dragon

I dream your passing in the night.
My soul would share that airy flight.
I too had wings, which brambles tore;
Feet fleet and light, now clogged with mire;
Once my eye too was sharp and bright.

Ah! Dancing feet that now must plod.
Ah! Airy soul, now tied to earth.
Ah! Mournful, sad and dreary eye
That white, black, colours, cannot see
But knows the world in shades of grey.

Now earthbound, yet I long to fly,
To raise my silent voice on high.
You pierce my heart with fiery sword.
My word yet binds me like a cord.
I try to weep. My tears run dry.

I keep a promise. Feel I must,
Though all seems long-since turned to dust.
Where shall I go? What shall I be?
Will you stoop down and rescue me?
Who from myself can set me free?

Huddled in the dark, afraid,
I long to follow where you lead.
I would make music; pluck the strings.
Oh, shelter me beneath your wings
And plant in me the dragon seed.

(January 2004)

Out Of Season

White the paper ere the first word was written.
Yours the hand that seeded the paper with symbols.
Meaning bloomed. Mysterious flowers, strange-scented,
Flourished bright petals.

Seeming spring stole swiftly in; hope dawned falsely.
Trust in bright appearances led me astray.
Eros softly, secretly undermined me.
Grief tipped his arrows.

White the air through which the first snowflakes drifted.
Red the blood, set coursing with sharp-tipped anguish.
Icy pain, insidious, deep inside me,
Battened upon me.

Yours the hand that unleashed the twisted bow-string,
Drove the darting pain; ripped the perfumed blossoms
Up by the roots; set cold ruin in the heart-space,
Bringing the death-wish.

If tears came on reading my words, would you tell me?
Hide the feeling, showing a mask untroubled?
Feelings hidden might as well be left unfelt.
Risk the exposure!

(February 2004)

Name-Dream

Half dreaming, half asleep, I was with you.
My head sank, seeking safety, on your breast.
Your arms, strong castle walls, encompassed me.
Your sapphire spells the midnight darkness blessed,
Transforming my black night,
Through your enchantment, to deep blue delight.

(April 2009)

Through The Desert

Long had I trod
On rock and stone,
Walking the desert path
Lonely, alone.

But now the arid way seems fair,
Since you are there,
Since we can share
The journey,
Find delight in it.

Now each sharp stone
Takes on a magic beauty of its own,
Blessed by your presence.

The way ahead
Awaits our feet.
You have my hand already - I am yours.
Shall you then take possession of your own?
Shall we set out together?

(April 2009)

Brush Fire

Dry grass
Sleeps in the sun,
Softly sighing.

Spark from nowhere.
Sudden field-fall.
Flames igniting.

Swift and hot
Through the summer meadow
Fierce fire flashes.

Grass, consumed,
Turns to ashes.
The bright fire passes.

(May 2009)

Tranquilidad

Paseando solo por la playa,
Mis pies en la arena mojada,
Oí el mar susurrando.
Mi cabeza lijera
Subió en el aire
Como una nube.
Ví el vuelo de pájaros blancos,
Y estaba tranquilo,
Acariciándote
Dentro de mi corazón.

(May 2009)

ICU

I see you, child, in love:
In this moment of waiting;
In this moment of meeting,
This moment of passion,
This time of contentment.

I see you too, my child,
In this moment of dying;
In this moment of birth,
In this moment of youth,
In this moment of age.

And I see the temple veil torn
And the earth unformed;
Watch the stars congeal,
See the snake
And the sun's dying flame.

(June 2009)

Ghazal

Alone, I think of you, I sigh, I pray,
I long for you, though you are far away.

I came to this strange land, seeking my love,
But found you not, for you are far away.

At night, behind closed eyes I dream of you
And think you near, though you are far away.

Waking, I send what messages I can,
Talking with you, though you are far away.

Always I feel your lack, the emptiness,
I am alone, and you are far away.

(Gaziantep, October 2010)

Seeking Safety

Fearful images I saw:
Cruel Taliban, dancing with joy,
Stoning young lovers.

Your family
Who, after me,
Should love you most,
Torment you with a future that would part us.

While governments seem spiders
Weaving wicked webs
To hold us trapped
And make us fit their patterns.

We twist and turn
Seeking only safety for our love:
Seeking a visa.

We met at times
- And some expense
We hold each other close,
We weep,
We part.

We jump through hoops
But no-one claps.

Who is our friend?
And where can we be safe?

(Karachi, January – February 2011)

Missing You

I wake in the night
My hands reach out
Missing your body

I wake in the night
Cold in the dark
Missing your warmth

I wake in the night
Ears strain in the silence
Missing your voice

I wake in the night
I muzzle the mattress
Missing your scent

I wake in the night
My body empty
Missing its soul

(Gaziantep, February 2011)

About the Author

Dr. John Ashdown-Hill is an historian, a Fellow of the Society of Antiquaries, a Fellow of the Royal Historical Society, a member of the Society of Genealogists, the Richard III Society and the *Centre Europeen d'Etudes Bourguignonnes*. He was Leader of Genealogical Research and Historical Advisor for the *Looking for Richard Project;* the rediscovery of Richard III's burial place in 2012. John was awarded an MBE in the 2015 Queen's Birthday Honours for his role in the project. John has written twelve history books and has numerous historical research articles published.
John lives near Colchester in Essex.

www.ingramcontent.com/pod-product-compliance
Lightning Source LLC
Chambersburg PA
CBHW030438010526
44118CB00011B/688